Alphathoughts

Alphabet Poems

by Lee Bennett Hopkins

Illustrations by Marla Baggetta

Wordsong
Boyds Mills Press

Published by Wordsong
Boyds Mills Press, Inc.
A Highlights Company
815 Church Street
Honesdale, Pennsylvania 18431
Printed in China

Publisher Cataloging-in-Publication Data (U.S.)

Hopkins, Lee Bennett.
    Alphathoughts : alphabet poems / by Lee Bennett Hopkins ; illustrations by
Marla Baggetta.—1st ed.
[32] p. : col. ill. ; cm.
Summary: Short verselike definitions of words from *A* to *Z*. Poems
include a word or words that begin with the letter featured.
ISBN 1-56397-979-9
1. Poetry. 2. Alphabet—Poetry.
I. Baggetta, Marla. II. Title.
811.54 21 AC CIP 2003
2002105847

First edition, 2003
The text of this book is set in Universe Bold Extended.

Visit our Web site at www.boydsmillspress.com

10 9 8 7 6 5 4 3 2 1

To Rebecca Kai Dotlich for *F*
—L. B. H.

For my mom, Peg
—M. B.

A

ALPHABET

A
miraculous
set of
twenty-six
letters
when
rearranged
makes
every
English
word
appear

B
BOOKS

Pages
and
pages
of
bound
forevers

CUSTODIAN

Keeper
of
clean

D

DOGS

With
wagging tails
they
breed
a more
delightful
world

E

ELEVATOR

A
box
to
easily
shuttle
people
up
and
down
and
down
and
up

F
FRIENDS

Never
apart—
even
when
far
away

G
GYMNASIUM

A place where girls' and guys' muscles race

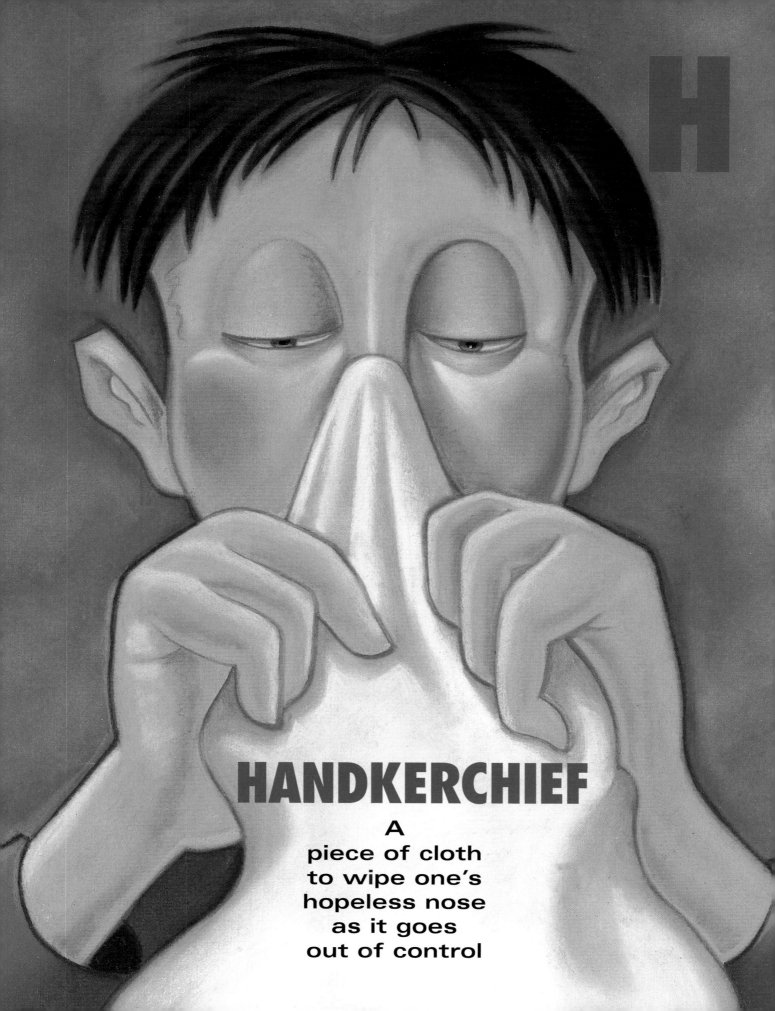

HANDKERCHIEF

A piece of cloth to wipe one's hopeless nose as it goes out of control

I

IGLOO

A
house
of
ice
to
keep
warm
in

J

JELLY

A
jolly
peanut-butter
playmate

K

KITCHEN

A
room
where
garlic
and
cupcakes
kiss

L

LIBRARY

A
pleasure place
to
ponder
lifelong
dreams

M

MASK

A magical disguise to make you feel like someone new

N

NACHOS

A crunch of culture within one nibble

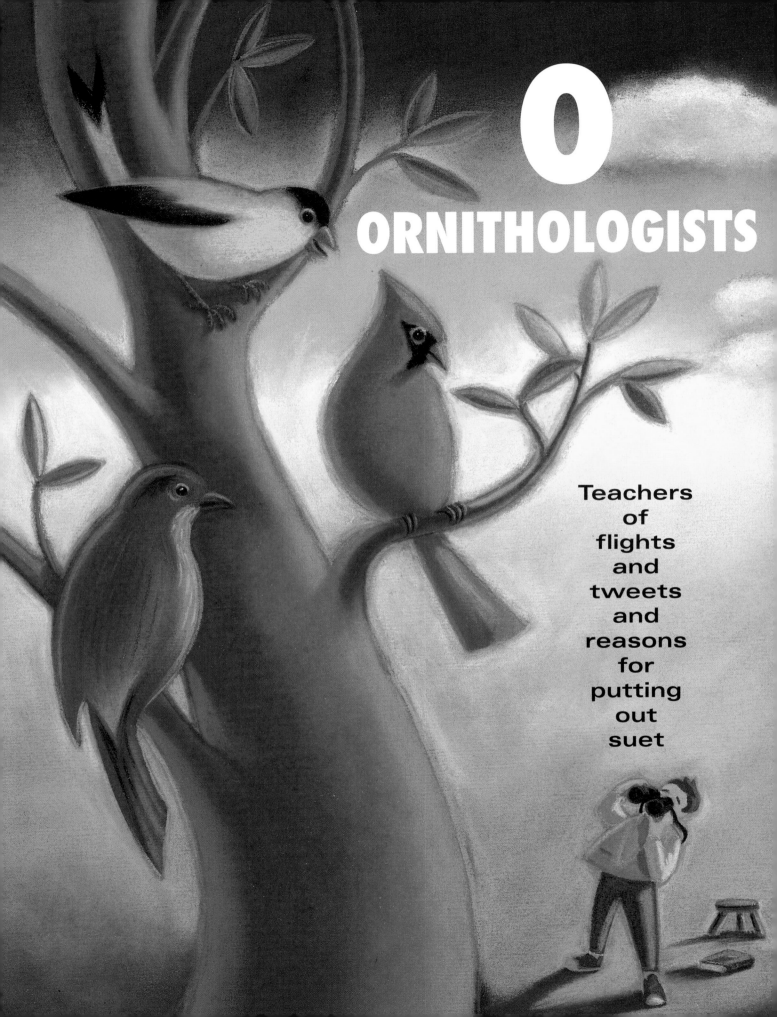

O
ORNITHOLOGISTS

Teachers
of
flights
and
tweets
and
reasons
for
putting
out
suet

P
PENCILS

Magical
implements
waiting
for
stories,
poems . . .
to
pop out
from
head
to
lead

Q

QUIET

Something
never
quite
enough
of

R
REUNION

A
coming together
to
remember
memories

S

SCIENCE

The way
the who
what
when
why
how
and where
surprisingly
get
us
there

T

TEACHER

One
who
touches
your
all-tomorrows

U

UNICORN

A
unique
fantasy
wanting
to
become
true

V

VERSE

Vibrant rhyme to stay close to you forever through time

Vibrant rhyme to

stay close

to you

forever through time

W

WIND

One
wild
thing
you
cannot
talk
back
to

X

X
marks
spots
kisses
(xxx)
and
winning
at
tic-tac-toe

Y

YARN

Hanks
of colors,
rainbow bound,
yearning
to become
a
knitted
some-
thing

ZOOS

Z

Where
animal-
and
people-
breath
zealously
mingle